PHILADELPHIA Phillies

BY K. C. KELLEY

The
Child's
World®

Published by The Child's World®
1980 Lookout Drive • Mankato, MN 56003-1705
800-599-READ • www.childsworld.com

Acknowledgments
The Child's World®: Mary Berendes, Publishing Director
Red Line Editorial: Editorial direction
The Design Lab: Design
Amnet: Production
Design Elements: Photodisc

Photographs ©: Gene J. Puskar/Shutterstock Images, cover, 1, 2;
Chris Williams/Icon SMI, 5; Scott Kane/Icon SMI, 6;
MacIntire Bros./Public Domain, 9; Frank Franklin II/AP Images,
10; Shutterstock Images, 13; Design Lab, 14; Philadelphia
Daily News/Zuma Press/Icon SMI, 17; AP Images, 18;
Christopher Szagola/Icon SMI, 21; Amy Sancetta/AP Images,
22; GRG/AP Images, 22 (inset); Aspen Photo/Shutterstock
Images, 25 (top); Zuma Press/Icon SMI, 25 (center); Rick
Seeney/Shutterstock Images, 25 (bottom); Brian Ekart/Icon
SMI, 26; Tim Vizer/Icon SMI, 27

ISBN 9781623239770
LCCN 2013947264

Printed in the United States of America
Mankato, MN
December, 2013
PA02188

ABOUT THE AUTHOR

K. C. Kelley has written dozens of books on baseball and other sports for young readers. He has also been a youth baseball coach and called baseball games on the radio. His favorite team is the Boston Red Sox.

Cover: Cole Hamels, Pitcher

CONTENTS

Go, Phillies!

Philadelphia is called the "City of Brotherly Love." It's also the City of Baseball Love! Phillies fans are some of the most loyal—and loudest—in baseball. They haven't had a lot of winning teams to watch over the years. In recent seasons, though, the Phillies have been one of baseball's best. And the fans certainly love that! Let's meet the Phillies.

Chase Utley congratulates a teammate on his home run.

Who Are the Phillies?

The Philadelphia Phillies are a team in baseball's National League (NL). The NL joins with the American League (AL) to form Major League Baseball. The Phillies play in the East Division of the NL. The division winners and two wild-card teams get to play in the league playoffs. The playoff winners from the two leagues face off in the **World Series**. The Phillies have won two World Series championships.

Laynce Nix follows through on his swing in a game against the Cardinals.

Where They Came From

The Philadelphia Phillies have been around for a long time. In fact, they joined the NL in 1883! They became the Phillies in 1890 and haven't changed their name since. No other Major League team has played that long with the same name and in the same city. In their first 67 years, they finished as a top team several times. In many other years, they were near the bottom of the NL.

The 1887 team also played their home games in Philadelphia.

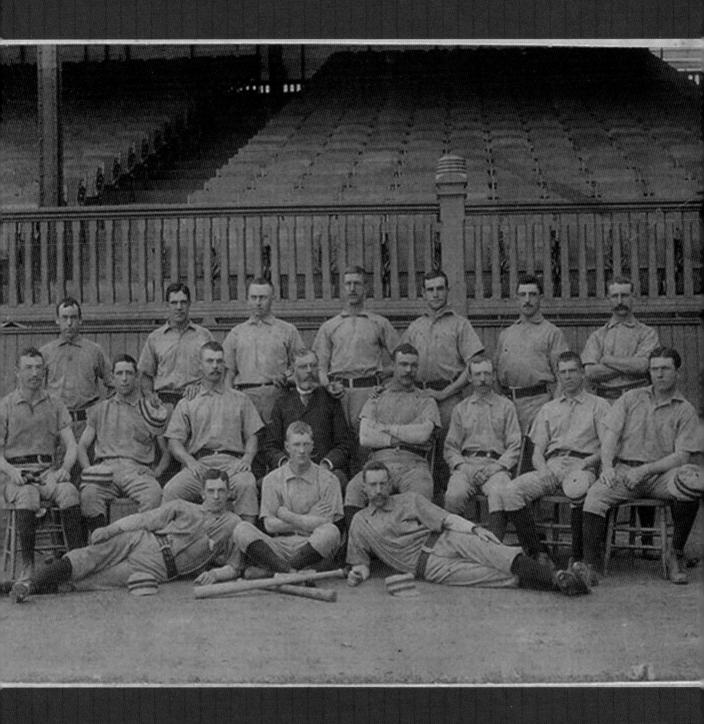

Who They Play

The Philadelphia Phillies play 162 games each season. That includes about 19 games against each of the other teams in their division. The Phillies have won 11 NL East championships. The other NL East teams are the Atlanta Braves, the Miami Marlins, the New York Mets, and the Washington Nationals. Philadelphia's games against the Mets are always exciting! The Phillies also play some teams from the AL. Their AL opponents change every year.

Chase Utley forces out a New York Mets player at second base.

Where They Play

Since 2004, the Phillies have played in Citizens Bank Park. Fans like it much more than their old home in Veterans Stadium. Citizens Bank Park has real grass, for one thing. And it was made just for baseball. At Veterans, the team shared the field with the Eagles football team. Outside the new ballpark, fans can visit statues of Phillies all-time favorites Richie Ashburn, Robin Roberts, Steve Carlton, Harry Kalas, and Mike Schmidt.

Phillies fans fill the seats of Citizens Bank Park to cheer for their team.

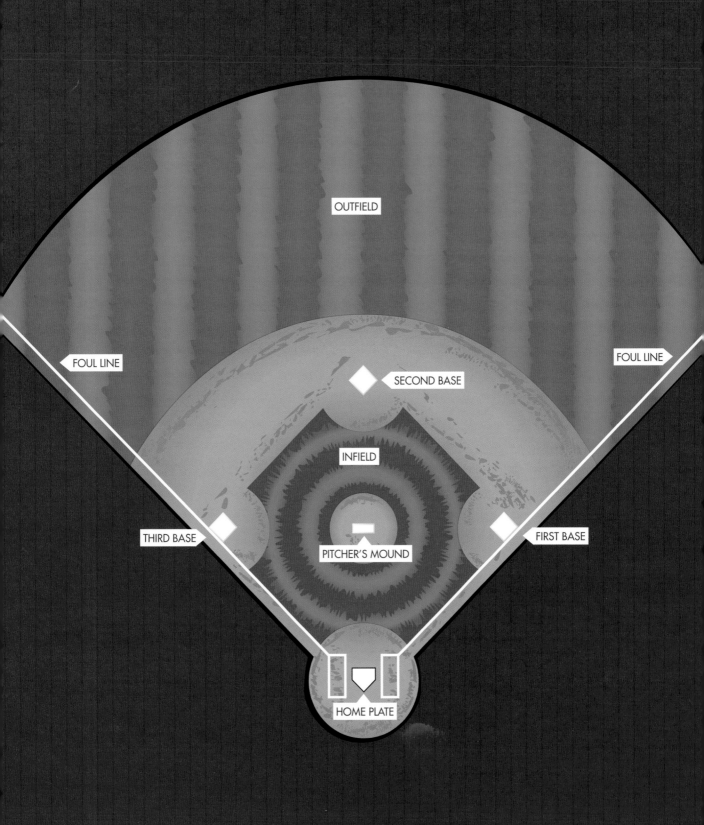

OUTFIELD

FOUL LINE

FOUL LINE

SECOND BASE

INFIELD

THIRD BASE

FIRST BASE

PITCHER'S MOUND

HOME PLATE

The Baseball Diamond

Baseball games are played on a field called a diamond. Four bases form this diamond shape. The bases are 90 feet (27 m) apart. The area around and inside the bases is called the infield. At the center of the infield is the pitcher's mound. The grass area beyond the bases is called the outfield. White lines start at **home plate** and go toward the outfield. These are the foul lines. Baseballs hit outside these lines are out of play unless they are caught by a fielder. The outfield walls are about 300–450 feet (91–137 m) from home plate.

Big Days

The Phillies have had some great seasons in their history. Here are three of the best:

1915: *After 32 years, the Phillies finally won an NL championship. They lost in the World Series to the Boston Red Sox. The Sox were led by a pitcher named Babe Ruth.*

1980: *Finally! After nearly 100 years in the NL, the Phillies won their first World Series.*

2008: *This year's Phillies had slugging power and great pitching. They beat the Tampa Bay Rays in five games to win their second World Series.*

The Phillies celebrate their victory in the 2008 World Series against the Rays.

Tough Days

Not every season can end with a World Series win. Here are some of the toughest seasons in Phillies history:

1923: *The Phillies have had some bad stretches. This was one of the worst. They finished at the bottom of the NL. It was their fourth last-place finish in five years!*

1964: *The Phillies led the NL by six games on September 18. Less than two weeks later, they had lost the lead—and their chance at the World Series. The season was known as the "Philly Flop."*

1973: *The Phillies finished in last place in the division . . . for the third season in a row!*

The 1964 Phillies team was leading the NL before the "Philly Flop."

Meet the Fans

Phillies fans are famous for their booing! They can be tough on teams that don't do well, but they love teams that win! The fans went crazy in 2008 when their team won baseball's biggest prize. They greeted their World Series champs with a huge parade through downtown. The biggest Phillies fan of all is a giant, green . . . thing! Since 1978, the Phillie Phanatic has been one of baseball's most famous **mascots**.

The Phillie Phanatic is a fan favorite. He gets the fans to cheer loud.

Steve Carlton, Pitcher

Heroes Then . . .

Chuck Klein was a star slugger for the Phillies in the 1930s. He won the **Triple Crown** in 1933. In the 1950s, pitcher Robin Roberts was one of baseball's best. In the 1960s, slugger Dick Allen was one of the top home run threats. The best Phillies player of all time was Mike Schmidt. This **Hall of Fame** third baseman hit 548 home runs from 1972 to 1989. He also won ten **Gold Gloves** for defense. Phillies pitcher Steve Carlton won four **Cy Young Awards**. In 1972, he won 27 games. All the other Phillies pitchers together only won 32!

Mike Schmidt was the best all-around player for the Phillies.

Heroes Now . . .

The Phillies have a mix of players who helped them win the 2008 World Series and new young stars. Slugging first baseman Ryan Howard was the NL **Most Valuable Player (MVP)** in 2006. He reached 200 home runs in fewer games than any player in baseball history! Shortstop Jimmy Rollins was the 2007 NL MVP. He's a great team leader and a terrific base stealer. Second baseman Chase Utley is a five-time All-Star. Outfielder Domonic Brown emerged as a star in 2013. Lefty Cole Hamels is the pitching ace. He was the MVP of the team's 2008 World Series win.

The present-day Phillies are loaded with star players.

Ryan Howard, First Base

Domonic Brown, Outfield

Cole Hamels, Pitcher

BATTING HELMET

TEAM JERSEY

BATTING GLOVES

TEAM PANTS

BAT

BASEBALL CLEATS

26

Gearing Up

Baseball players all wear a team jersey and pants. They have to wear a team hat in the field and a helmet when batting. Take a look at Ryan Howard and Carlos Ruiz to see some other parts of a baseball player's uniform.

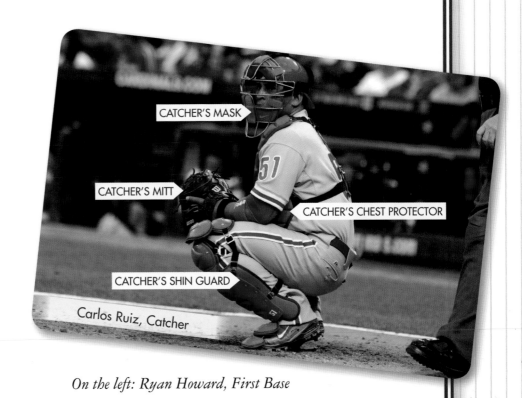

CATCHER'S MASK

CATCHER'S MITT

CATCHER'S CHEST PROTECTOR

CATCHER'S SHIN GUARD

Carlos Ruiz, Catcher

On the left: Ryan Howard, First Base

Sports Stats

Here are some all-time career records for the Philadelphia Phillies. All the stats are through the 2013 season.

THE BASEBALL

A Major League baseball weighs about 5 ounces (142 g). It is 9 inches (23 cm) around. A leather cover surrounds hundreds of feet of string. That string is wound around a small center of rubber and cork.

HOME RUNS

Mike Schmidt, 548
Ryan Howard, 311

RUNS BATTED IN

Mike Schmidt, 1,595
Ed Dalahanty, 1,286

BATTING AVERAGE

Billy Hamilton, .361
Ed Delahanty, .348

STOLEN BASES

Billy Hamilton, 508
Jimmy Rollins, 425

WINS BY A PITCHER

Steve Carlton, 241
Robin Roberts, 234

WINS BY A MANAGER

Charlie Manuel, 1,000

EARNED RUN AVERAGE

George McQuillan, 1.79
Grover Alexander, 2.18

Glossary

Cy Young Awards awards given to the top pitcher in each league. Steve Carlton won four Cy Young Awards.

Gold Gloves awards given to the top fielder at each position in each league. Mike Schmidt won ten Gold Gloves.

Hall of Fame a building in Cooperstown, New York, where baseball's greatest players are honored. Third baseman Mike Schmidt is in the Hall of Fame.

home plate a five-sided rubber pad where batters stand to swing. Runners touch home plate to score runs.

mascots a person in costume or an animal that helps fans cheer for their team. The Phillie Phanatic is a famous mascot.

Most Valuable Player (MVP) a yearly award given to the top player in each league. Ryan Howard was MVP in 2006.

Triple Crown an award given to the player who leads a league in home runs, RBI, and batting average in the same season. Chuck Klein won the Triple Crown in 1933.

World Series the Major League Baseball championship. The World Series is played each year between the winners of the American and National Leagues.

Find Out More

BOOKS

Buckley, James Jr. *Eyewitness Baseball*.
New York: DK Publishing, 2010.

Stewart, Mark. *The Philadelphia Phillies*. Chicago:
Norwood House Press, 2008.

Teitelbaum, Michael. *Baseball*. Ann Arbor,
MI: Cherry Lake Publishing, 2009.

WEB SITES

Visit our Web page for links about the Philadelphia Phillies
and other pro baseball teams: *www.childsworld.com/links*

*Note to Parents, Teachers, and Librarians: We routinely verify our
Web links to make sure they are safe and active sites. So encourage
your readers to check them out!*

Index